The Stories about Collecting happiness

NAME:

____

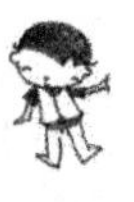

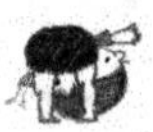

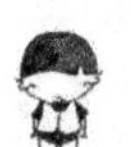

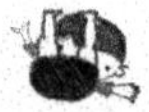

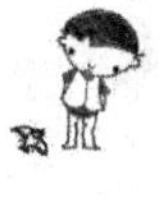

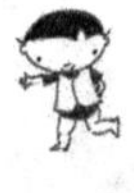

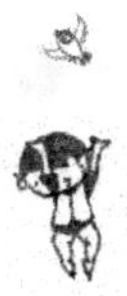

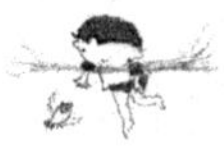

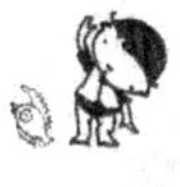

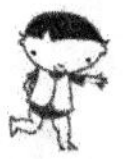

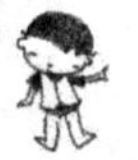

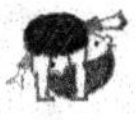

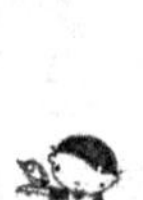

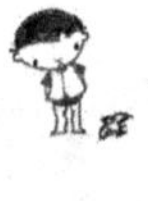

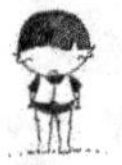

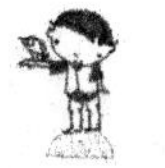

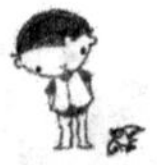

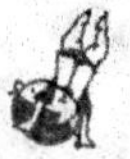

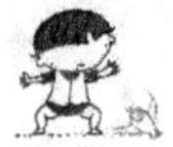

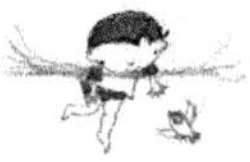

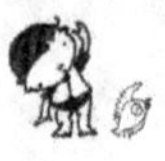

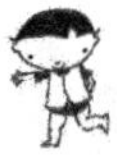

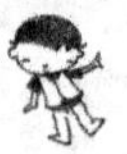

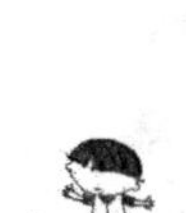

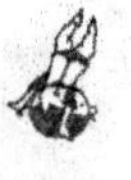

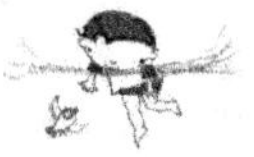

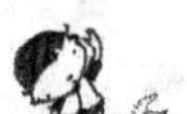

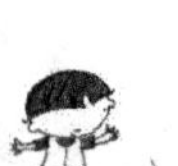

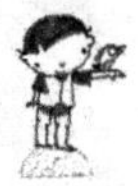

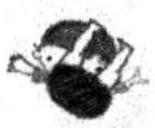

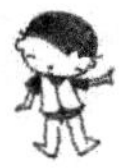

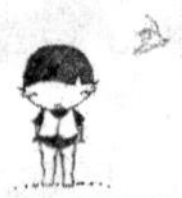

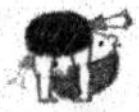

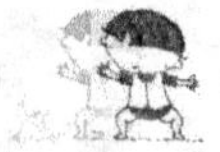

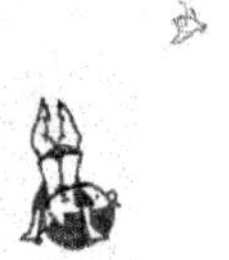

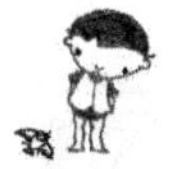

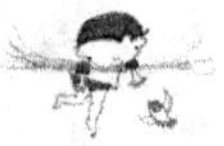

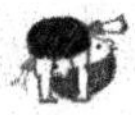

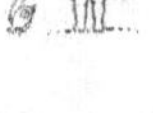

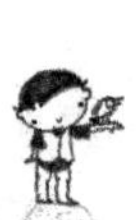

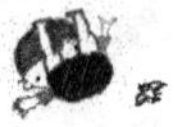

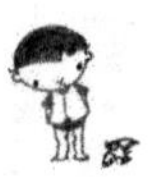

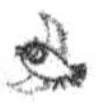

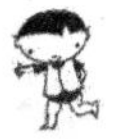

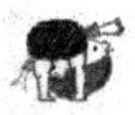

Happiness is a butterfly ,

which when pursued is always just beyond your grasp,

but which if you sit down quietly ,

may alight upon you .

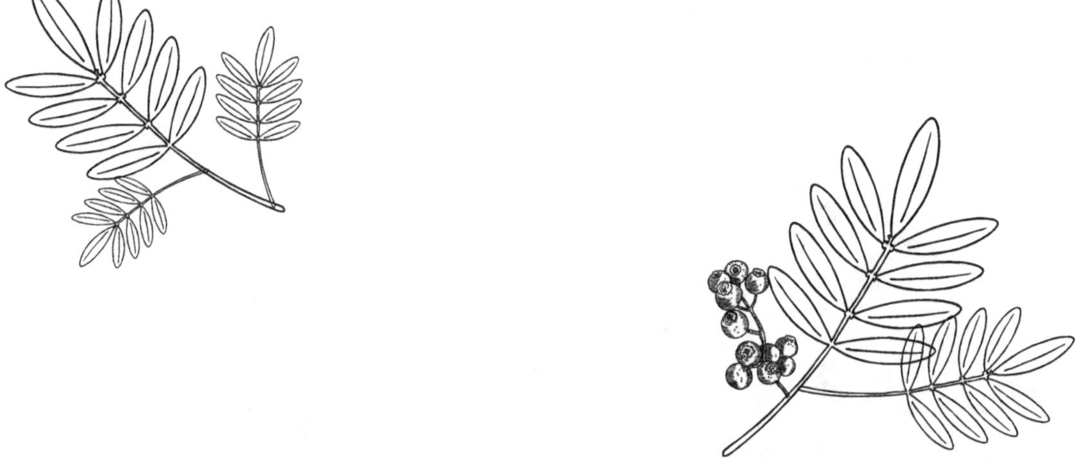

www.ingramcontent.com/pod-product-compliance
Lightning Source LLC
Chambersburg PA
CBHW080603220526
45466CB00010B/3238
9781677047406